MILK and COFFEE

———— ❖ ————

poems by
Patrick W. Flanigan

illustrations by
Christine Crozier

Pacific Grove Publishing

Text Copyright © 2002 by Patrick W. Flanigan
Illustrations Copyright © 2002 by Christine Crozier

Typography: Dave Christensen

Printed in the United States of America
by Cypress Press, Monterey, California

Published by:
Pacific Grove Publishing
P.O.Box 803
Pacific Grove, CA 93950
Telephone (831) 755-1701
Fax: (831) 375-4749

1 3 5 7 6 4 2

IBN 0-9668952-5-8

Also of interest
SURVIVING THE STORM
Poems by
Patrick W. Flannigan

For my wife, Anita, my Muse
Your intellectual curiosity made this book possible

CONTENTS

The Glen 1

Silence 2

While Shopping 3

The Mystic 4

The Spring Garden 5

Moles 6

The Mouse 7

Courting 8

Imagination 9

She Likes to Knit 10

Some Things Are Special 11

Now 12

Moonlight 14

Raising Canaries .16

Layers 18

The Meditation Room 20

Milk and Coffee .21

The Grandmothers Visit 22

Sometimes Words Flow 23

Sea Voices 24

Tasks 26

Meditating 27

Imaginary Friends 28

The Party 29

Reading Kafka 30

Untold Stories 32

Coming to America 33

Voices 34

Signs 35

The Hat 36

The Jacket 37

I Give Advice 38

I Have Loved 39

The Heavy World 40

The Shoppers 42

The Fall from Grace 44

Fountains 46

Ashes 47

Plant a Tree 48

After His Death 49

THE GLEN

The restless water
or some violent movement
deep within the earth
made a cleft in the rocks
ages ago.

Now, in that space,
green ferns breathe
the moist air,
redwoods stand
tall and silent,
a stream speaks
of distant snowy peaks
and caresses
the trout living
in its mossy pools.

I sat a long time
not knowing
what to say
about such a place

then I left
quiet and at peace.

SILENCE

Silence comes in many forms—

the shut up, squelched speechlessness
of the brow beaten and battered;

the mute body of an injured child,
head bandaged, breath driven by a machine;

the still, airless tomb
that has not heard birdsong
for a hundred years;

the noiseless, distant stars
sending us faint specks of light
from fires that burned
before the earth was born;

the inner peace at the center of our souls
that can be sensed only when we are quiet.

WHILE SHOPPING

He had forgotten about his soul
until he saw the sign that said
"Full and Part Time
Career Opportunities Available
Inquire Within"

He spent the rest of the day
inquiring within
until he heard a faint voice
that told him
slow down,
listen more,
stoop to look
into the eyes of children,
have a nice day
and come back real soon.

THE MYSTIC

Today in the garden
while I read
about monks and mysticism,
a chocolate colored butterfly
with orange stripes
and two white spots on its wings
landed on the shoulder
of a stone statue
of the Buddha
a few feet from my chair.

The butterfly just sat.

For that moment
in that place
books were not needed
to understand
monks, mysticism,
and the Mystery
that defies description.

THE SPRING GARDEN

In spring the garden is full of surprises.

Wind blown seeds sprout
in the crevices of brick paths.
Forgotten bulbs push green leaves
and white, blue, and yellow flowers
out of the dark, moist earth.
Skeletal twigs and branches
burst forth with yellow-green leaves
and fragrant pink and white blossoms.
Dark green pines add new pale tufts
to growing branches.

Birds and bugs,
singing and quiet things,
flying and crawling things
share our joy
in the spring garden.

MOLES

When was the last time
you thought about moles?

Today, walking in a birdsong filled forest,
seeing the sun on distant meadows,
hearing the voices of the wind and waves,
I felt solid ground
become spongy and soft.

Moles had lifted up the earth
going from an unknown place
to somewhere else.
Pressing through the soil
were they enjoying
the darkness and silence
as much as I
the light and sounds?

THE MOUSE

Something rustled the leaves nearby
and started to chew on leaf or twig.
It was not a white stag
nor a unicorn
nor a tiger burning bright.

It was a small brown mouse,
a creature like us,
trying to live life grandly.

COURTING

Two young men,
boyhood chums,
shaving imaginary beards
at least once a week
court budding maidens
using the words
of long dead poets.

Ancient passions
proclaimed to red, red roses
now withered
and turned to dust
stir in new hearts.

Reading words
with mock bravado
and fervor
modern swains
seek gentle laughs
and soft kisses.

IMAGINATION

She said:
Sometimes,
when my husband
plays the piano,
I imagine
he is serenading me.

It makes me
sing in the kitchen,
smile at the children,
and blush
when he looks
into my eyes.

SHE LIKES TO KNIT

My wife likes to knit.
She says it is relaxing.

She has made
scarves, sweaters, and shawls.

Today she is bringing
blue, white, and tan yarns
together in thin lines
like those places
where endless waves
wash upon
endless grains of sand.

I think she knits
to relax,
to bring order
to undisciplined threads,
and to create
beautiful things
that contain her love
when she gives them away.

SOME THINGS ARE SPECIAL

Some things are special—

the beauty revealed
when her dress
slips from her shoulders
and falls to the floor,

the smoothness of her skin,
the faint smell
of jasmine or honeysuckle
in her hair,

the power and passion
of her body and soul
when they are naked,
unrestrained,
given over to love
and lovemaking,

the joy of moments
remembered
and yet to be.

NOW

Some people
spend a lot of time
thinking about Eternity
when moments will dissolve
into one unending
stream of consciousness

but I like to think
about Now.
I mean this moment
or maybe the next,
with this color
in the sky,
this scent
in the wind,
this hand
on my shoulder

and the Now
when your breasts
are near my face,

your nakedness
meets mine,
and we make time
dissolve.

I like to think
about the thousands of Nows
that might occur
before I have to think about
Eternity.

MOONLIGHT

She likes to see
the full moon rise,
silver or amber,

to see that faint color
in the night sky
before the first arc
of intense light
peeks above the horizon,

to stand in awe
of Nature's quiet beauty
and repetitive generosity.

I like to share
those moments with her,
not so much to see
that bright disc in the sky
or its light
on the land or water,

but to see
its light on her face
illuminating the beauty
that is there today
and reminding me
of the first time
I saw her smile.

RAISING CANARIES

My wife raises canaries.

Some are yellow,
others orange,
several have dark wings
like the wild birds
that forage in the garden,
a few have tufts of feathers
on their heads
like ill fitting toupees.

They can be messy
scattering seeds and feathers
and producing more droppings
than such small creatures
should be able to make.

But they do fill the house
with song
and remind us that once
we raised children
and still know how
to be patient, gentle,
and willing to sacrifice
for others
who may or may not
know how to say
thank you.

LAYERS

Scientists call it
sedimentary rock,
the product of patient settling
onto the ocean floor
where time and pressure
push silt and particles together
until they let go of their individuality
and become part of vast sheets of stone
layered one on top of the other.

Here, at the foot of a cliff
on the edge of a continent,
those multihued layers
do not rest horizontally
as they had been formed.
They point straight up
toward the heavens
as if in prayer or meditation
trying to forget
the rage and wrath
that wrenched them ·
from the sleepy ocean bed.

I sit on a water worn boulder,
too full of doubt to pray,
too restless to meditate,
trying to remember
the songs my mother sang
when I was a child.

THE MEDITATION ROOM

They called it a chapel,
a meditation room,
this small wood building
perched on a cliff
above the ocean,
but he knew better.

He could smell the chickens
that had roosted
in this very room
when it was part
of Grandma's garage.

How it had moved from Indiana
he did not know
but he would not be fooled.
He would find
the cherry tree
just outside the door
and have a piece of pie
with ice cream tonight.

MILK AND COFFEE

Do you like
a lot of milk
in your coffee?

I mean
a lot of milk
the way Grandma
made it
when I was a small boy,
the way it would not
stunt your growth,

the way I make it now
when I want to remember
her face
and the joy
of her laughter.

THE GRANDMOTHERS VISIT

The summer my sister was born
both grandmothers came to stay
at the same time.

They came to see the new baby,
welcome her to the tribe,
and help my mother.

One was rotund, jolly,
and called me Patty.
The other, lean, stick-like,
seldom called me by name.

Each had different ways
of doing things
and the thin, quiet one
went outside
to rehang the wet laundry
after the one who sang
while she worked
had done it
all wrong.

SOMETIMES WORDS FLOW

Sometimes words are rhymed and precise
Sometimes words are hard and cold like ice.

But sometimes words flow
like a mountain stream
rushing from granite, snow capped peaks
around and over water worn boulders
tumbling as silvery, splashing waterfalls
stopping to rest in moss walled,
gravel bottomed pools
and then hurrying down to the green, grassy
plain below.

Sometimes words flow too swiftly
cutting through layers of soil and silt
revealing ancient bones
best left undisturbed.

SEA VOICES

A wall of granite
rises above the water
protecting a small cove
from the persistent movement
of a restless ocean.

In the base of the rock
a weakness
or a willingness
to compromise or submit
has produced a long tunnel.

With the tides
water flows
through the opening.
During storms
a rumble echoes
over the cove
and its rocky beach.

Tourists and scientists
say it is just the waves
but I have listened carefully
and I have heard the voices
of an ancient sea god
and drowned sailors.

TASKS

A crow carrying a pine cone
larger than its body
flapped its black wings
as it flew among the trees.

Others called out
hoarse encouragement
fluttering from branch
to leafy branch.

The effort seemed enormous
but meaningless
as I turned back
to the blank page before me.

MEDITATING

The young monk
sat for hours
trying to quiet
the monkey in the mind.
He sought to experience
Nothing.

He could not escape
the aches in his back,
the sound of his father's voice,
the smell of new cut grass.

He felt and thought
without relief
while I held a pen,
stared at blank paper,
and could think only of
Nothing.

IMAGINARY FRIENDS

This morning,
less than six years old,
she bobbed in the water
of the country club pool
talking to herself
or an imaginary friend.

This afternoon,
age hidden by grime,
he pushed a grocery cart
in the city streets
talking to himself
or an imaginary friend.

This evening,
grey appearing in my hair,
I wrote short poems
on thin sheets of paper
talking to myself
or an imaginary friend.

THE PARTY

In an afternoon spent this way
there must be a poem.

Maybe it's the woman in purple
with the hoop earrings
and the silver polish
on her toenails
or the man in the Panama hat
with the sunglasses
and the belly
hanging over his belt.

Or it could be me
holding a glass of white wine,
talking to strangers,
and wondering
there must be a poem
in an afternoon spent this way.

READING KAFKA

His brain flooded with inspiration and exploded splattering the walls with partially formed thoughts. His wife, who heard the noise and came running into the room, was saddened to tears but also felt a conflicting inner joy—I told him to stop reading Kafka.

Yes, she had told him to stop reading Kafka and he had ignored her. He insisted on dangerous experiments with words and ideas. Once he had combined two mixed metaphors on a piece of notebook paper and almost started the house on fire.

Another time, he tried to find a rhyme for orange and had to be heavily sedated and kept in a dark room for three nights and seven days. His friend Buzz told him to only try to rhyme words like heart and fart, dime and time, car and far. For a while, he took that advice to heart and would burp instead of fart, saved every dime, always stayed on time, and drove his car everyday, but not very far.

Even the best advice can be forgotten or ignored and, indeed the suggestions of both

Buzz and his wife suffered that fate. Just as surely fate would have it that on the seventh day of the seventh month in the year of 1977, he opened the cover of Kafka's METAMORPHOSIS and began reading in German and in English. Three hours and twelve minutes later his wife heard the explosion and the rest is history.

Fortunately some of the ideas were fresh enough to be scraped off the walls and preserved on parchment and fine vellum, later to be turned over to atheistic scholars, who, banned from working on the Dead Sea Scrolls, sought the challenge of trying to figure out the content of his brain at the time of the big bang.

His wife fell in love with one of the scholars named Ned. Although they never went to bed, they occasionally went to the floor or the back seat of his Renault. Ned was able to charm her with his innocent smile and a quotation he had located on the ceiling directly over where her husband had blown up.

Life went on.

UNTOLD STORIES

The veins
on the old man's
thin arms
were like the blue
back roads on a map
of a lonely country.
The creases
on his face
were like canyons
carved by smoky clouds,
sun, and wind.

He called me "sonny"
and asked for a light.
I was too young
to care about his story
and he was too old
to remember.

COMING TO AMERICA

The tent canvas flapped
against ropes and poles.
Smoke, steam, and crimson sparks
rose from the campfire.

Ancestors—men, women, children—
holding the railings of sailing ships
or crowded below deck
in lumbering steamers

appeared in dreams
coming to America
sometimes as angels,
sometimes as birds of prey.

VOICES

Have you ever heard voices?

Not the voices of people in your house,
or passing by the window,
or coming from the radio or television

but voices like the terrible one
that told Abraham
to kill his only son
or the faint one heard reluctantly
by the prophet Samuel

or the voices heard
by some murderers and saints
instructing them to do great evil or good.

Would the world be a better place
if it were silent, mute, devoid of sound?

Could I live without the singing
of my wife's canaries,
the pugnacious cries of the hummingbird,
the laughter of children,
the sound of my voice or yours
saying I love you?

SIGNS

A sparrow falls,
an owl's beak rips
into the soft belly of a mouse,
an old woman's back bends
and does not straighten,
a blind man trips on the stairs.

The priests and preachers
say You are still alive
but I am filled
with fear and trembling.

Let me feel Your warm gaze
on my neck,
hear Your breath
moving through the trees,
and find Your tears
among the raindrops.

THE HAT

A stranger passed by
wearing a hat

an old man's hat

like my father's,
like the one
he gave me
for Christmas,
the one I wear
in the garden
to protect me
from the sun.

I do not look good
in that hat
but I am starting
to feel comfortable
in it.

THE JACKET

The jacket I wear everyday
contains threads of joy and sorrow
woven in patterns
I do not always understand.

I do know that it is mine
because I was there
when the fabric was woven
and felt the smoothness
of the silk
and the coarseness
of the wool
and the sharpness
of the needle.

If I took off the coat
I might understand its patterns
and appreciate its meaning
but then what would protect me
from the cold
and hide my nakedness?

I GIVE ADVICE

I am paid to give advice—-
how to live and sometimes
how to die,
how to accept help
or how to be the gentle hand
that caresses a brow
or empties a bedpan.

We all play roles—-
doctor, nurse, patient,
family, or friend.

Yet we are made
of the same
sinews, muscles, veins.
Our hearts do not beat differently
because of different race or ancestry.

We all rise out of
and settle back into
the same dust and silence.

We all are part
of a Mystery
that is sensed only rarely
but is present
always.

I HAVE LOVED

There are people I have loved,
not like a wife or mother,
not like a father or sister,
but loved none the less

for they have trusted me
to work for their well being.
They have sought the protection
of my knowledge and skill.

They have asked me
to be near at the hour of crisis
or at the moment
of silent surrender.

Some of them still visit
for a checkup, a handshake,
or a hug.
Others only wait

in an unknown place
for the day when I, too,
will move toward
a great white light or nothing.

THE HEAVY WORLD

The world is a heavy place
of stone and water
resting on the shoulders of Atlas
or carried on the back of a turtle
or called forth from the great void
by a whirlwind God
who rested after six days of labor.

The world is a heavy place
with windstorms and fires,
avalanches and earthquakes,
floods and great waves
that threaten
to blow us away,
bury us without celebration,
or wash us into unfathomed depths.

The world is a heavy place
of strife and hate and killing
based on color or creed,
tribe or ancestor.

Ancient wrongs
real of imagined
drive us
to curses and destruction,
sorrow and tears.

The world is a heavy place
but the courage of a blade of grass,
the hope of a flower,
or your smile
remind me
that it does not rest
on my frail shoulders.

THE SHOPPERS

The organically grown golden delicious apple sitting on the refrigerator shelf reminded me of yesterday's trip to the local health food store. The rows of certified organically grown fruits and vegetables, the boxes and bags of dried or "naturally processed" foods, the herb teas and spices, the bottles of vitamins and minerals and cure-alls or cure-somethings were in their usual places. The scents and oils and lotions and "how to" and "how not to" books were in their usual places. Even some of the semiorganic, tie-dyed, mild to moderately worried customers were in their usual places.

The memorable sight that the apple brought to mind, however, was that of two unusual health food store customers. Two young, muscular black men in black shoes, black pants, black shirts, and black bandanas were at the check out counter buying fruits and snacks. They did not look like gang wannabes. They looked like the real thing. Real people whose lives were surrounded by danger and drugs and violence. Whose lives were threatened by AIDS and cops and bullets from passing cars.

They looked like real people who knew sorrow and anger. They looked like people who could rob a store to help support a drug habit or to express their outrage at injustice so common it is commonly ignored.

And yet there they were in my local store seeking safety from pesticides and preservatives. They were seeking longevity and health while dressed in a fashion that pointed to lives destined for abrupt and untimely ends beyond the reach of organically grown papayas.

THE FALL FROM GRACE

He did not know
exactly when it happened,
when he fell from grace,
when he was no longer
one of the chosen few.

Maybe it started that day
when he drove through a puddle
sending a sheet of muddy water
onto a man sitting in a wheelchair
waiting for a bus.

It was an accident
but he still laughed
and thought poor bastard
as he looked through
the rear view mirror.

Maybe it started years ago
when he was too busy
to change a diaper
or notice the smoothness
of his wife's skin.

Maybe it started only today
when he forgot
where he was going
and why he had gotten
into the car.

But it had happened
and he sat alone
in a shiny Mercedes
without a penny in his pockets,
without a hand to hold.

FOUNTAINS

I like fountains
especially in gardens
where the sound
of moving water
carries on a breeze
that stirs leaves and flowers.

Today that breeze
also carries the sound
of a distant bell
tolling to mourn someone
who also may have loved
the sounds of moving water
and the sights and scents
of a garden.

I do not know
his or her name
but I do know
the value of this moment,
the beauty of this place,
and the meaning
of gratefulness.

ASHES

When I die
wait for a windy day
and carry my ashes
to a rocky point
that juts into the sea.

Scatter those ashes slowly
to mix
with the air, water, and earth,
to become one
with the fishes,
the shore birds and sand fleas,
and the yellow flowers
that cover the meadow
every spring.

Years from now
listen for my voice
in birdsong,
look for my face
among the leaves of the oak,
and know
that I move
in the depths of the ocean.

PLANT A TREE

When I die
plant a young tree
over my grave.
Do not call it
a sapling.

With time
you or your children
or a weary traveller
can rest in its shade.
Someone may find
a poem or simple message
among its leaves.

When the wind, lightning,
or a steel blade
bring this tree down,
touch the growth rings
at its core
and know that someone
loved this world
and thought of you
before he died.

AFTER HIS DEATH

His depression lifted
and he fed the roses
growing over his grave.

It did not happen
the first year after his death
but it did happen

and the world was a better place
because of his generosity
and the beauty it produced.